Mitsubishi A6M5 Model 52 Zero

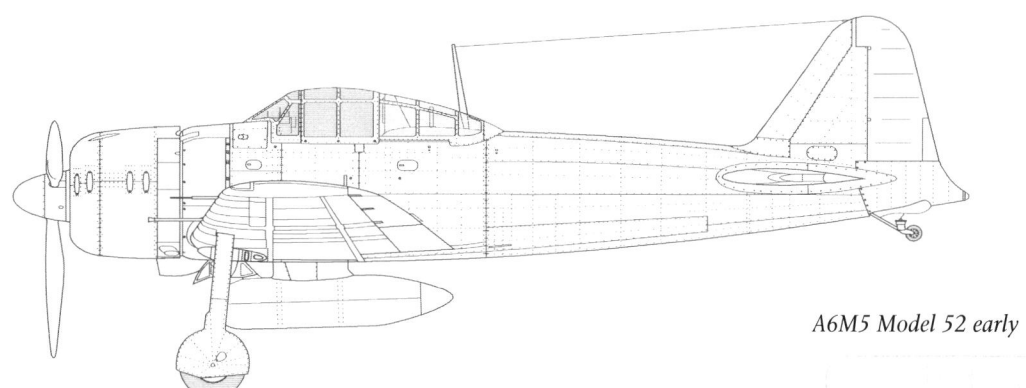

A6M5 Model 52 early

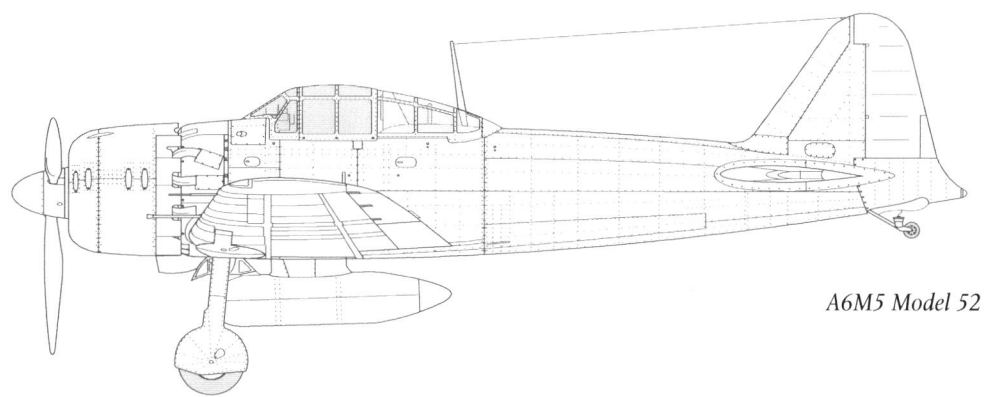

A6M5 Model 52

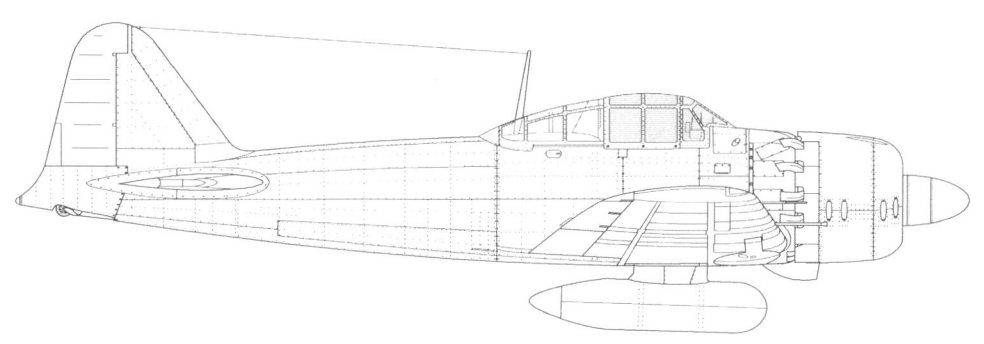

A6M5 Model 52 with large spinner

1/72

Drawings: Dariusz Karnas

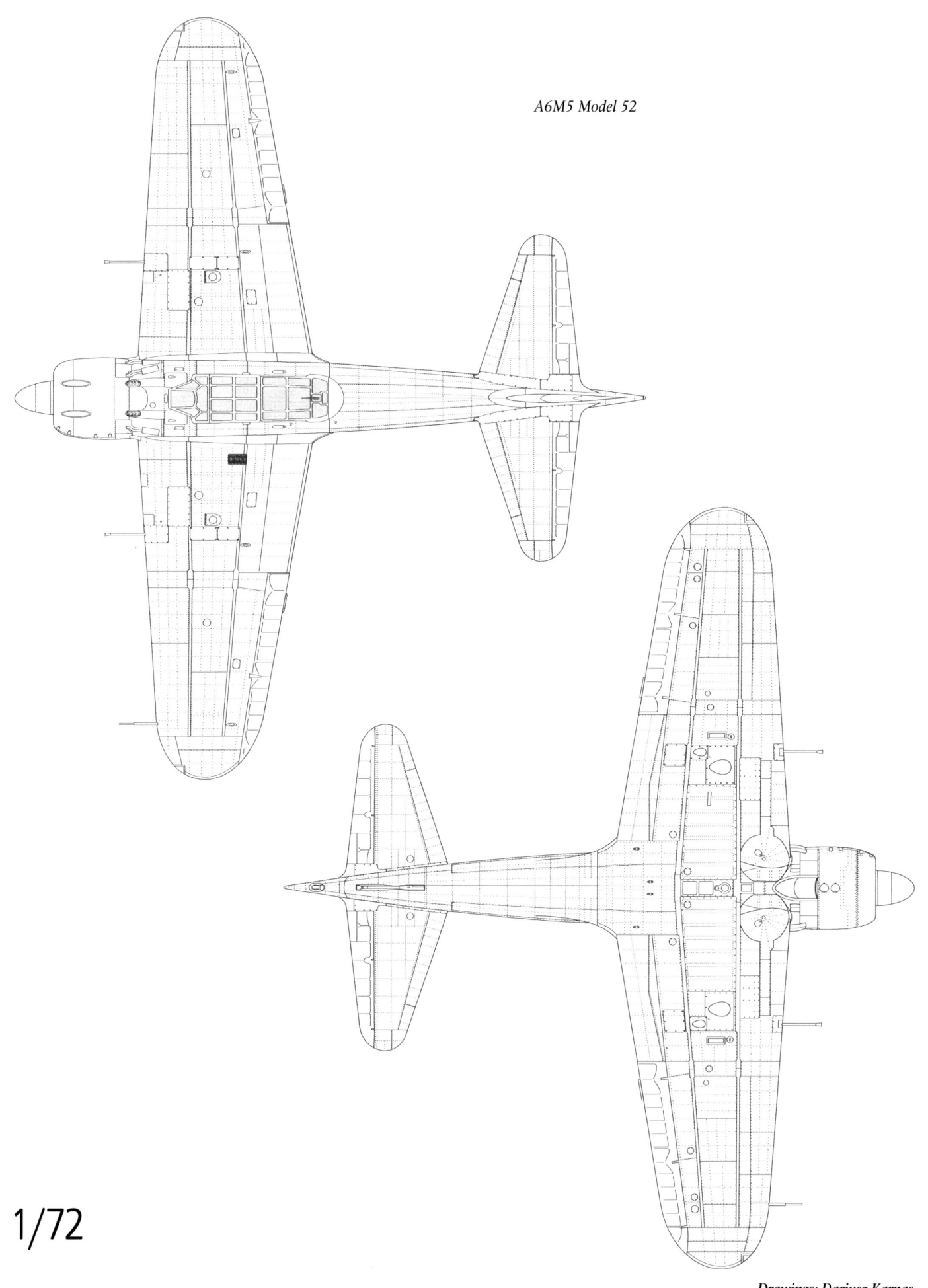

A6M5 Model 52

1/72

Drawings: Dariusz Karnas

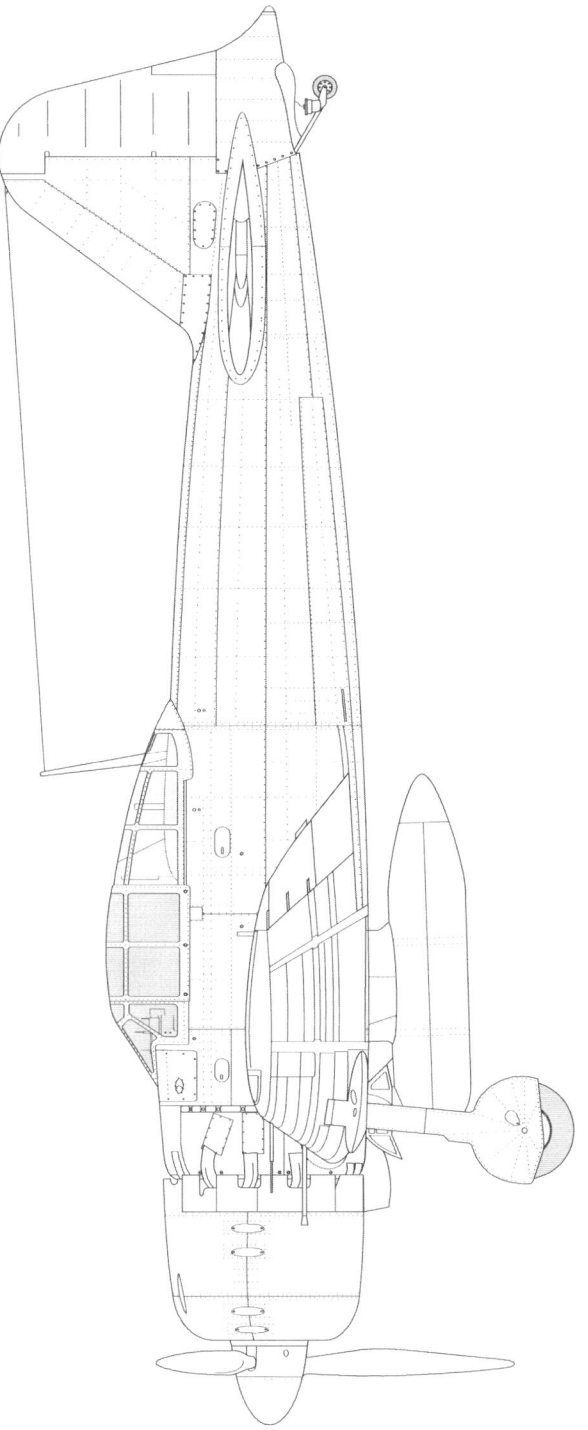

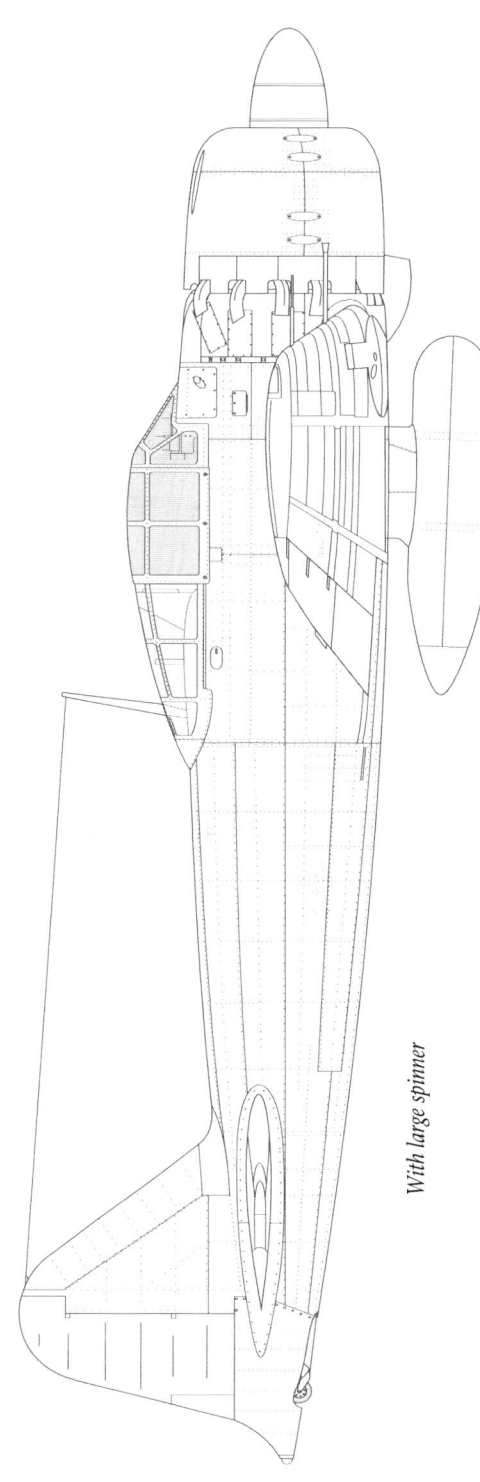

A6M5 Model 52

With large spinner

1/48

Drawings: Dariusz Karnas

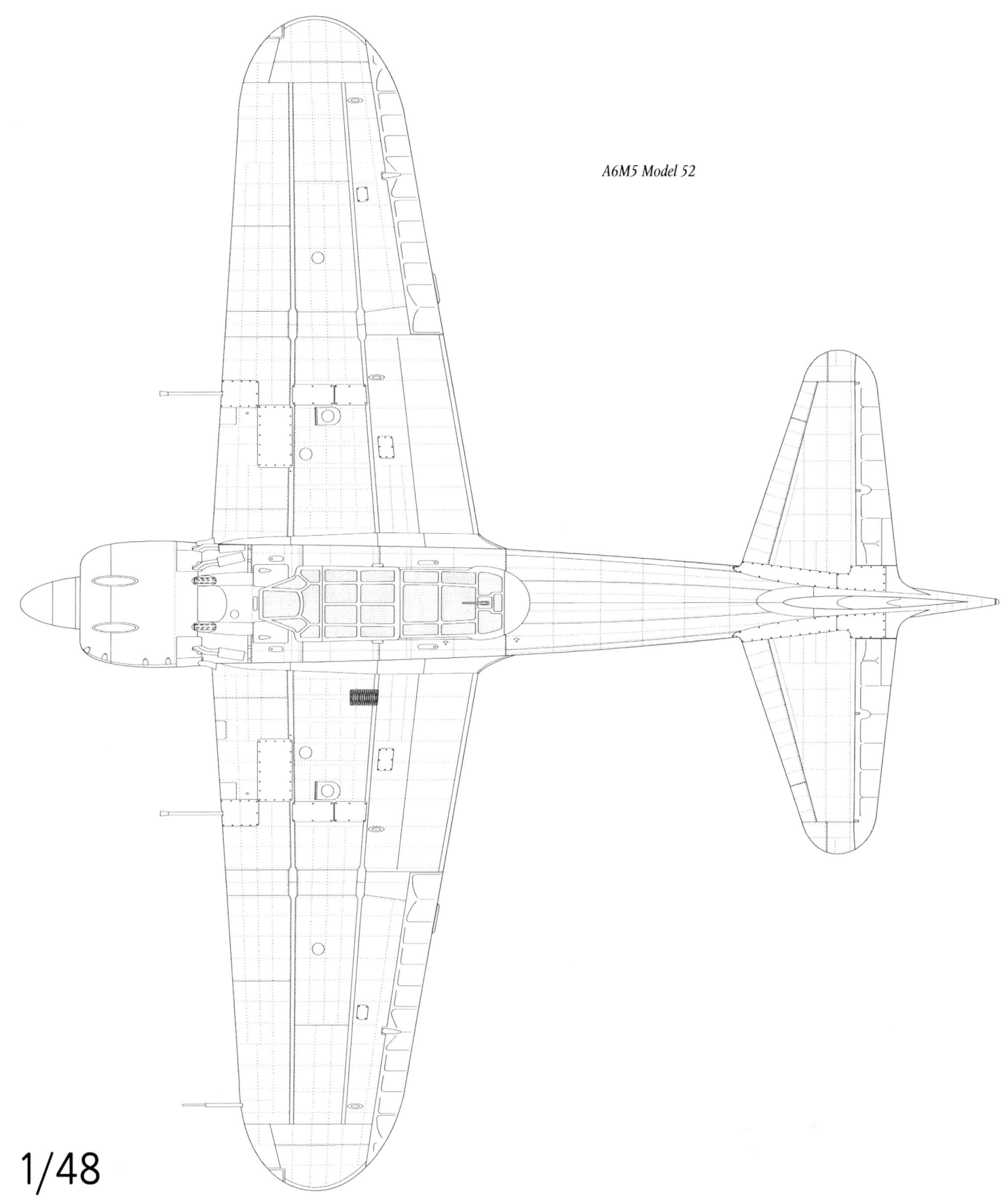

A6M5 Model 52

1/48

Drawings: Dariusz Karnas

A6M5 Model 52

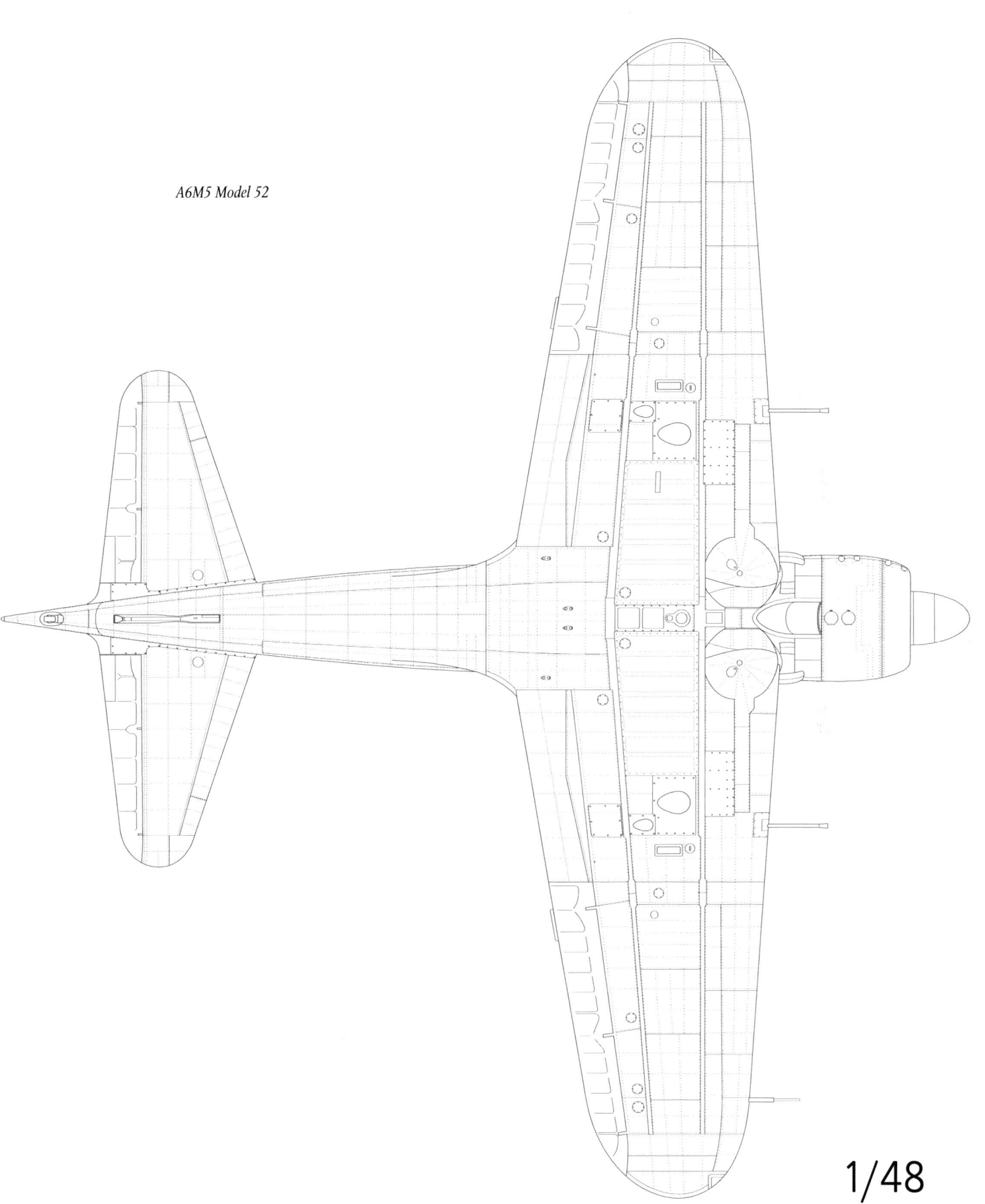

1/48

Drawings: Dariusz Karnas

A6M5 Model 52 in American Markings, TAIC 29. Aircraft during test flights in USA, 1944/45. (A. Lochte coll.)

A6M5 Model 52 found by American troops at Saipan, Marian Islands. (US National Archives)

Above: A6M5 Model 52 at turn. Details of the underside are shown. Photos of the under surfaces are not very common.

Right: A6M5 in the USA ready to be tested. Clearly visible is the American Star under the right wing.
(Both A. Lochte coll.)

Engine cowling of A6M5. Note separate exhaust pipes and redesigned fuselage gun outlets.

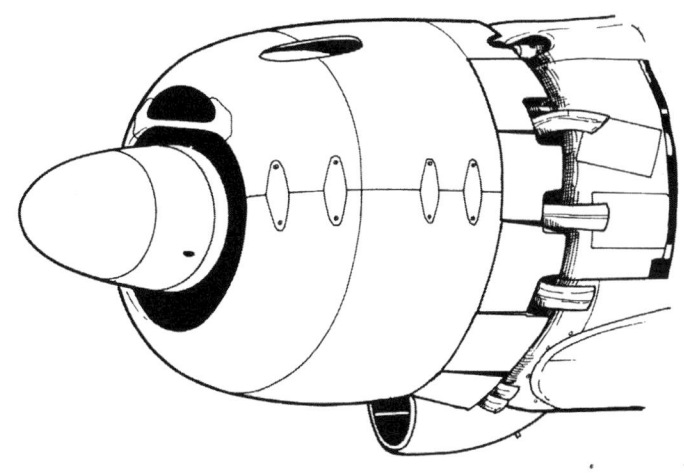

A6M5 Model 52, c/n 5357 (built by Nakajima), tail No. 61-120, found at Saipan. Aircraft preserved in Planes of Fame Museum, Chino, CA, USA. (A. Lochte)

Bottom: *Side view of A6M5 Model 52. Aircraft preserved in Chino. (A. Lochte)*

Two photos of the A6M5 fuselage – cockpit section displayed in IWM, London, UK. This plane was captured at the end of the Pacific War. ATAIU-SEA markings were applied by the RAF in Malaysia. This Zero, along with other captured Japanese aircraft ended up at Tebrau Airfield and then transported by ship to the United Kingdom, where arrived in 1947. Its Sakae 21 engine is displayed separately at the Aerospace Museum at Cosford. (Photos R. Pęczkowski)

Port side of the A6M5. (All photos A. Lochte)

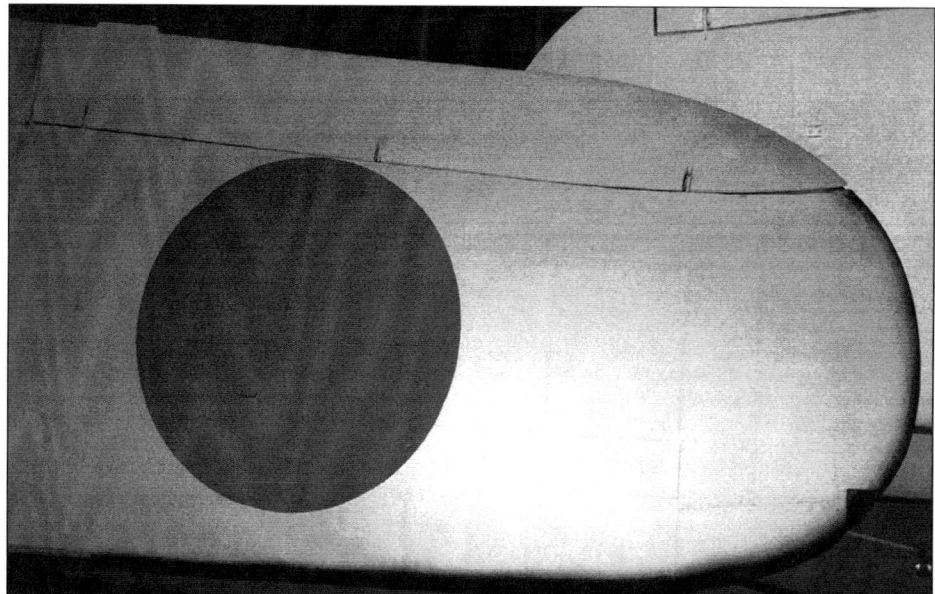

Starboard wing underside details, A6M5.

Port wing underside. Riveting is well visible.

Close up view of the aileron and the flap of A6M5. (All photos A. Lochte)

Underside of the port wing, A6M5. Aileron trim tab is visible.

Inner construction of the flap is shown.

Drawing of the flap construction and dimensions.
(Technical Manual)

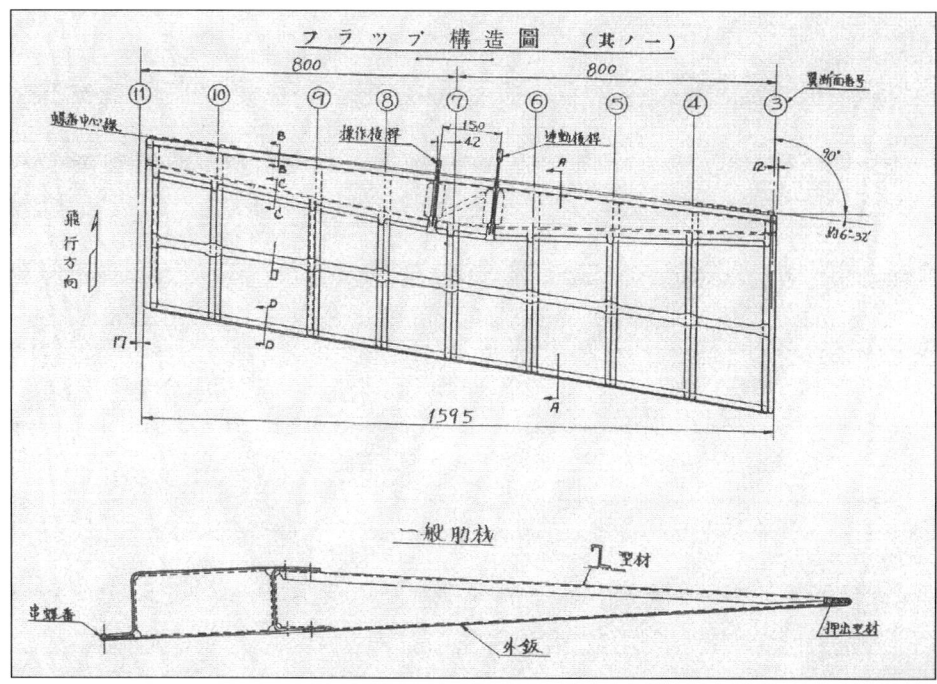

Outer part of the flap in open position.

Port side of the A6M5 canopy. Note also retractable foot steps marked in red on the fuselage.
(A. Lochte)

Starboard side of the A6M5 canopy.

Windscreen details and lock is visible.

Windshield, port side. Machine gun recharge handles are also visible.
(All A. Lochte)

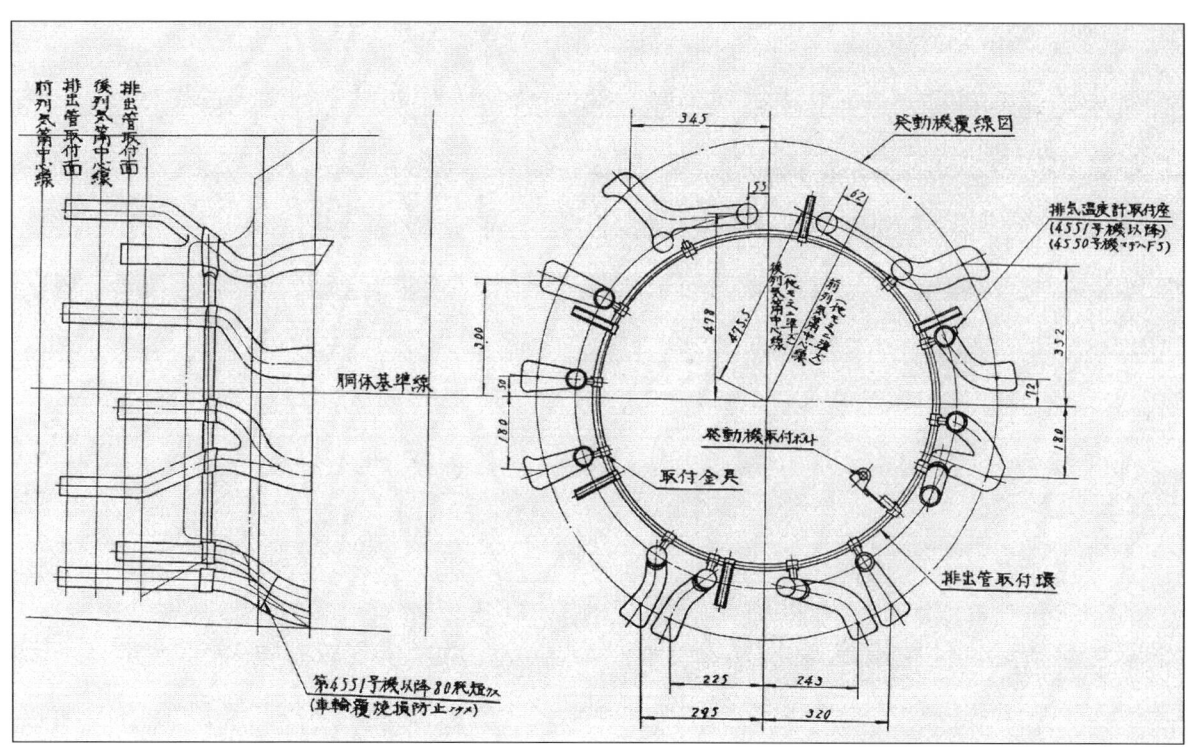

Exhaust pipes installed on A6M5 Model 52 and later models. (Technical Manual)

American soldiers checking spare Sakae 21 engine found at one of the Japanese airfields, Okinawa, 1945.

Four photos of the A6M5 Model 52 engine compartment preserved in Cosford, UK. (R. Pęczkowski)

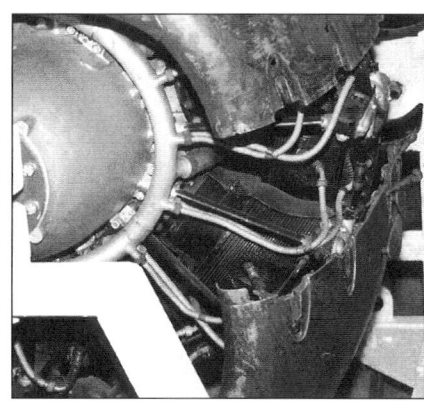

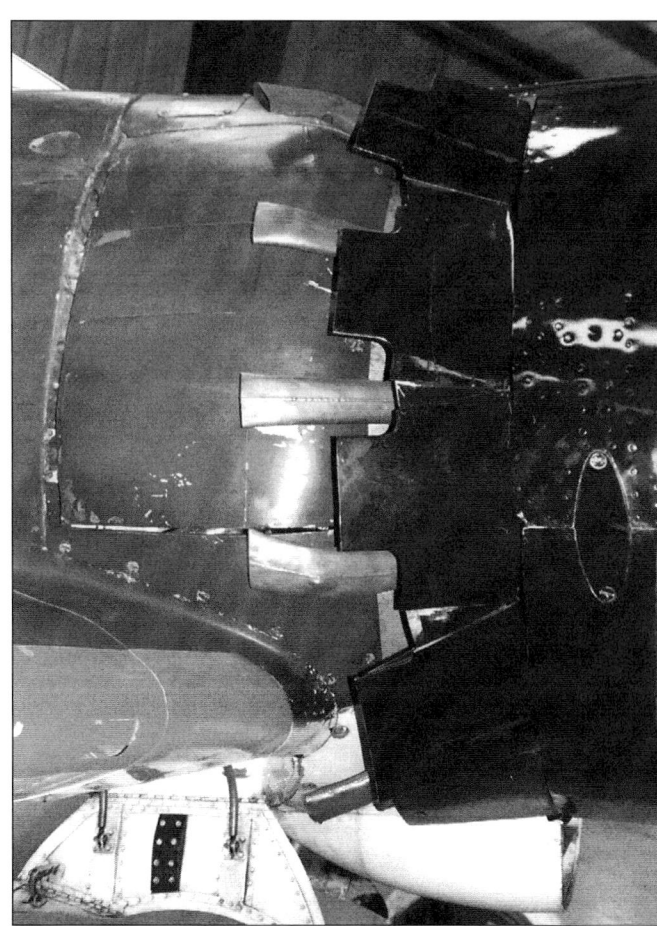

Three photos of the A6M5 engine cowling and exhaust pipes. Note the shape of the pipes. (All photos A. Lochte)

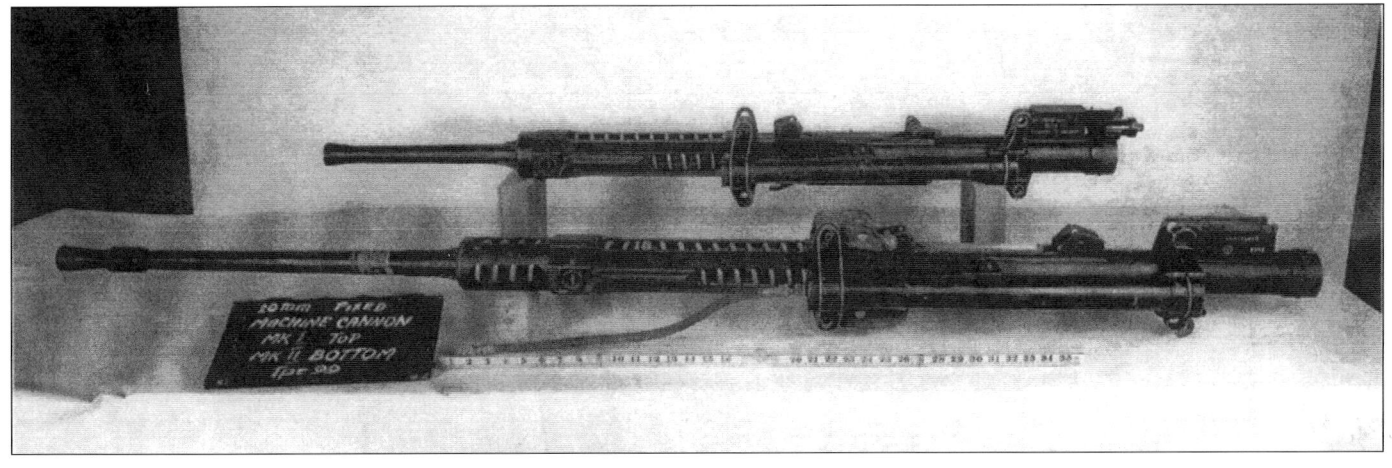

Cannon Type 99 Model 1, 20 mm and Type 99 Model 2, 20 mm. (US National Archives)

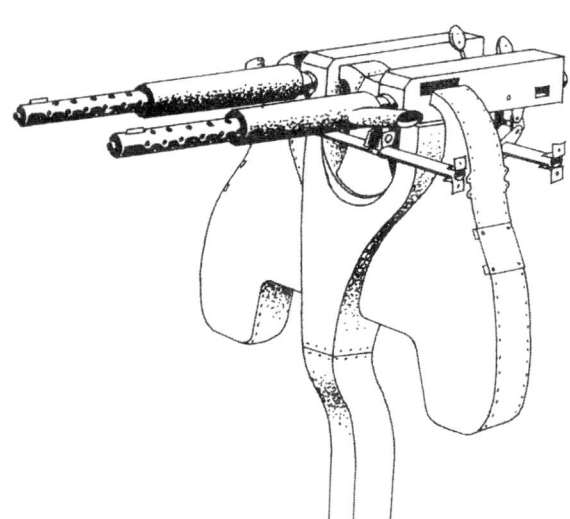

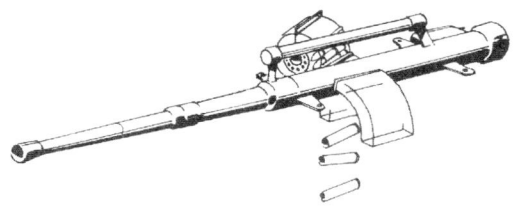

Above: *Cannon Type 99 Model 1 Mk 3, cal. 20 mm with drum magazine.*

Left: *Machine guns, Type 97 Model 3ko, cal. 7.7 mm.*

2.1. 主翼組立 縮尺 ¹/₂₀

寸法記入テキ個所ハ従来通リトス

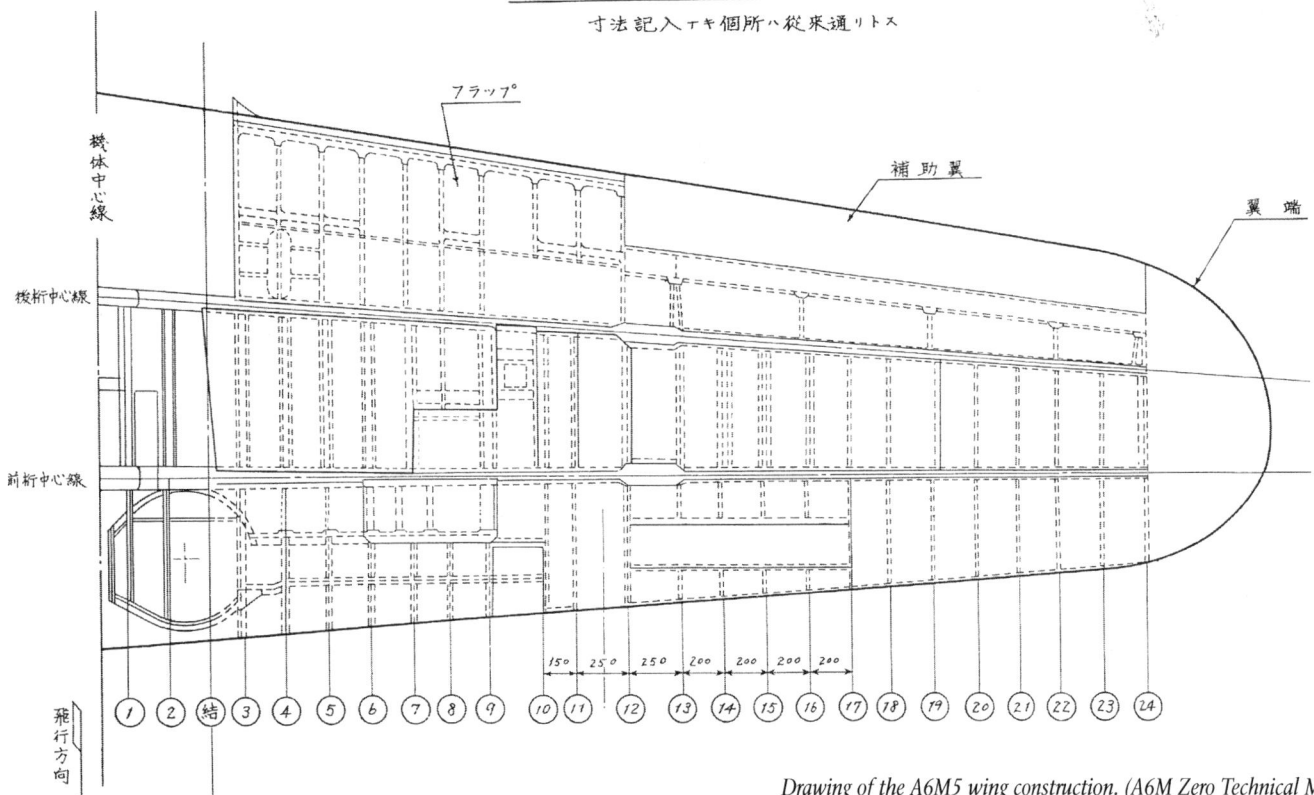

フラップ

補助翼

翼端

機体中心線

後桁中心線

前桁中心線

飛行方向

150 25.0 250 200 200 200 200

① ② 結 ③ ④ ⑤ ⑥ ⑦ ⑧ ⑨ ⑩ ⑪ ⑫ ⑬ ⑭ ⑮ ⑯ ⑰ ⑱ ⑲ ⑳ ㉑ ㉒ ㉓ ㉔

Drawing of the A6M5 wing construction. (A6M Zero Technical Manual)

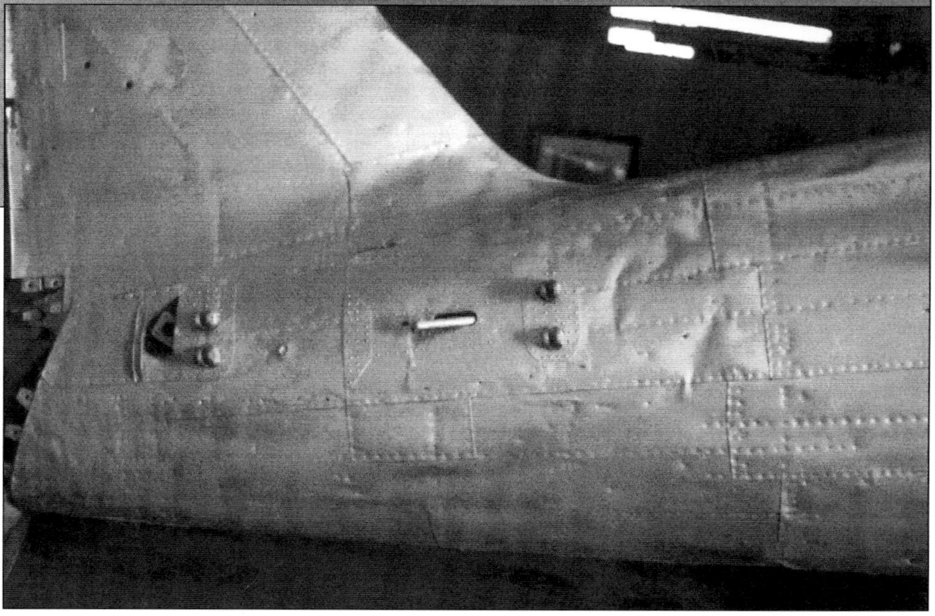

Above: Captured, tested by the Americans A6M5. Tail shape is well shown.
(US National Archives)

Right: Rear part of the fuselage with horizontal stabilizer removed. Mounting points are visible.
(A. Lochte)

Main wheel and wheel hub. Brake pipe is also visible. (A. Lochte)

Restored A6M5 Model 52 in flight. Zero wing shape is clearly shown. (S.T. Hards via J. Kightly)

A6M5 engine cowling, Separate exhaust pipes are visible. (A. Juszczak)

Main wheel and wheel hub. Brake pipe is also visible. (A. Lochte)

Photos of the tailwheel. Note the fork leg details and 150x75 mm tyre. (Both photos A. Lochte)

Hisato Nakada

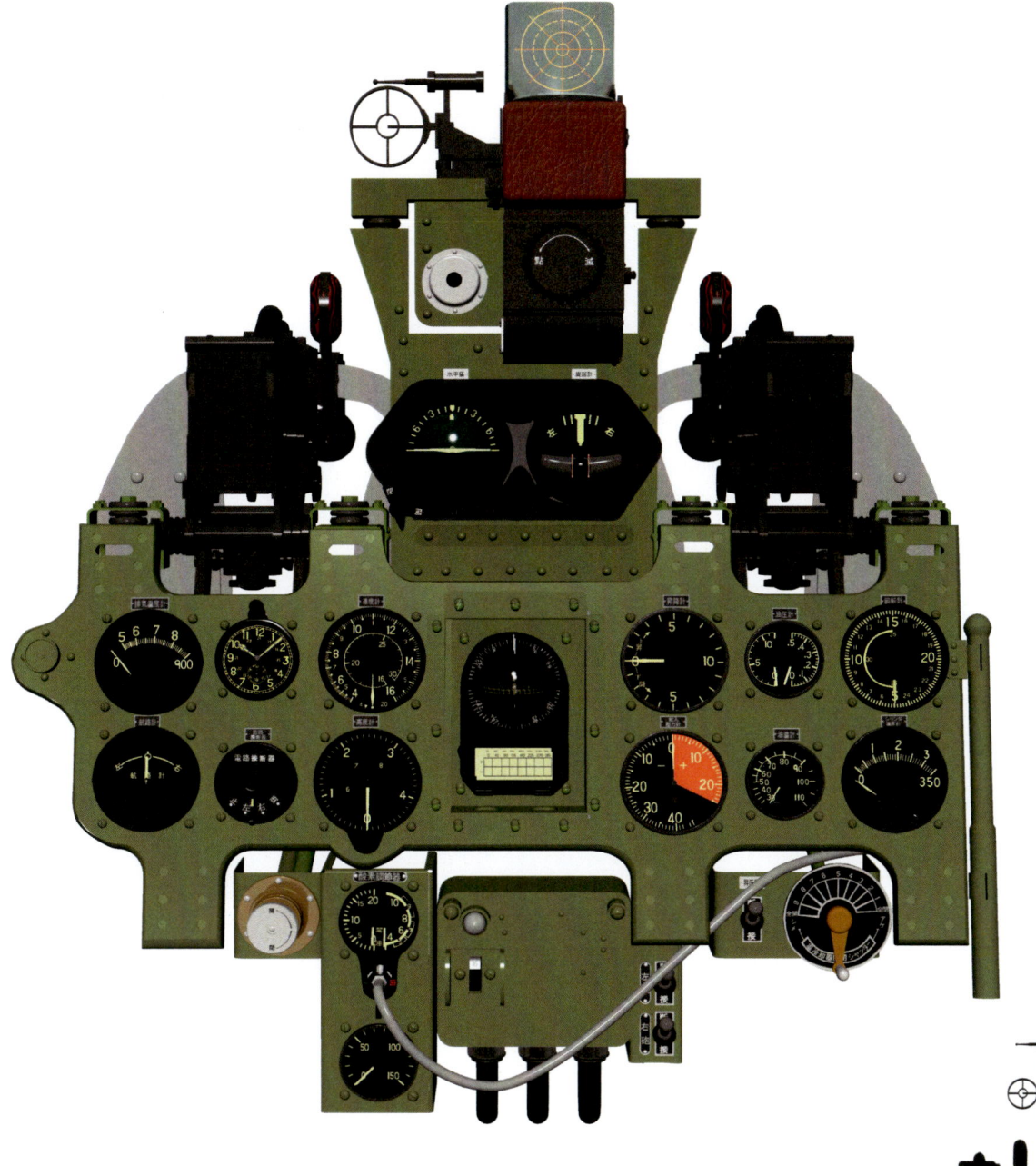

1. Artificial horizon, Model-2
2. Turn and bank indicator, Model-2
3. Emergency boost control
4. Exhaust gas temperature gauge, Model-1
5. Chronometer
6. Air speed indicator, Model-3
7. Magnetic compass, Type 92, Model-2
8. Rate and climb Indicator, Model-1
9. Fuel and oil pressure gauge, Model-1, Mk.2
10. Tachometer, Model-1
11. Cylinder head temperature gauge, MK.1
12. Oil temperature gauge, Model-1, Mk.1
13. Manifold pressure gauge, Model-2, Mk.1
14. Altimeter, Model-3
15. Engine magneto switch
16. Radio direction finder
17. Engine primer fuel pump
18. Oxygen flow regulator, Model-2
19. Hydraulic pressure gauge, Model-2
20. Fire control master switch
21. Cannon loading switches
22. Ignition booster switch
23. Oil cooler door operating hand crank
A. Gunsight, Type-98, Model-1
B. 7.7 mm machine gun, Type-97 (Right only)
C. 7.7 mm machine gun, Type-97 (Left only)

A5M5 Model 52 (Nakajima built) of 261st Kokutai, captured at Saipan in 1944.

Zygmunt Szeremeta '20

Zygmunt Szeremeta '20

Zygmunt Szeremeta

22

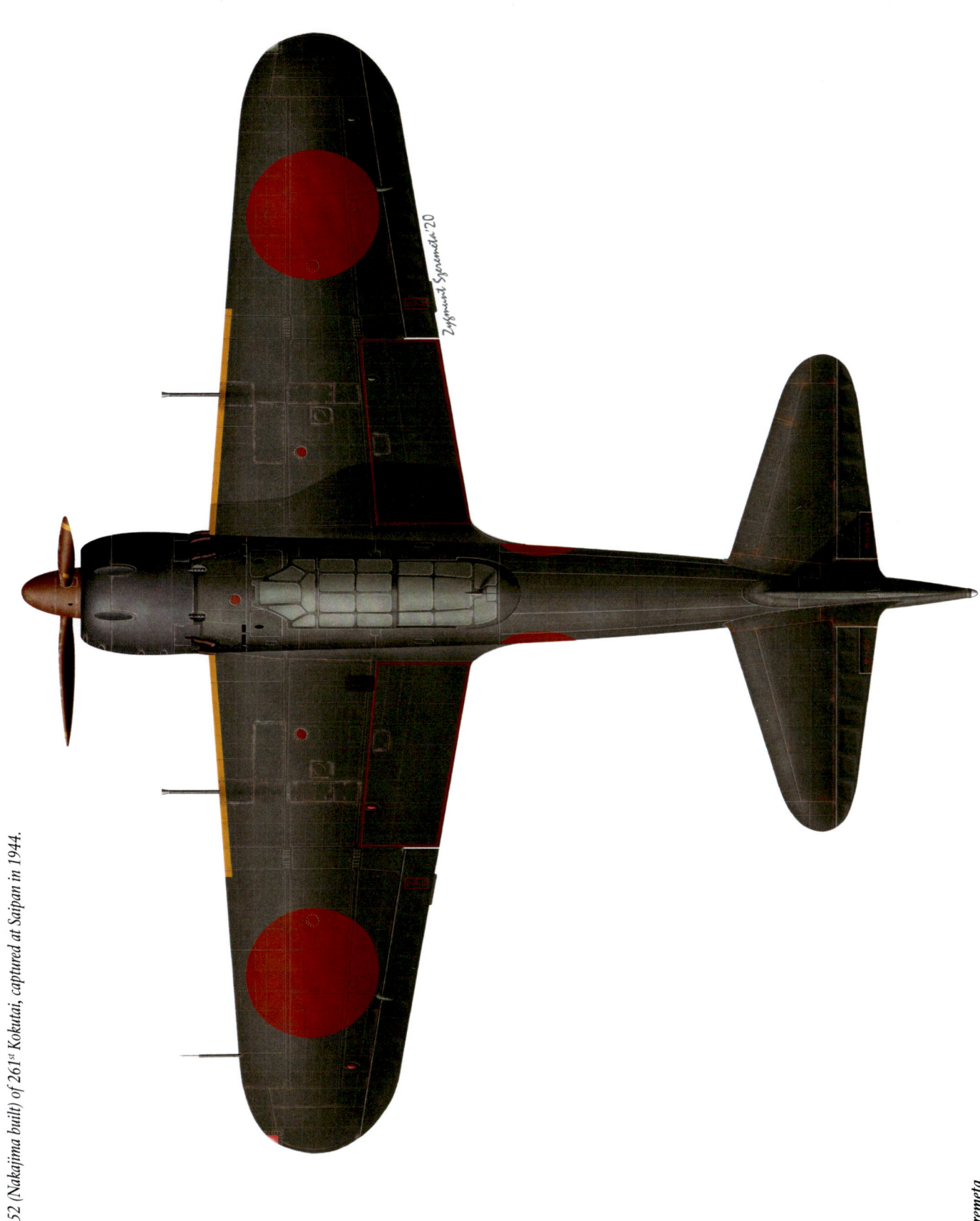

A5M5 Model 52 (Nakajima built) of 261st Kokutai, captured at Saipan in 1944.

Zygmunt Szeremeta

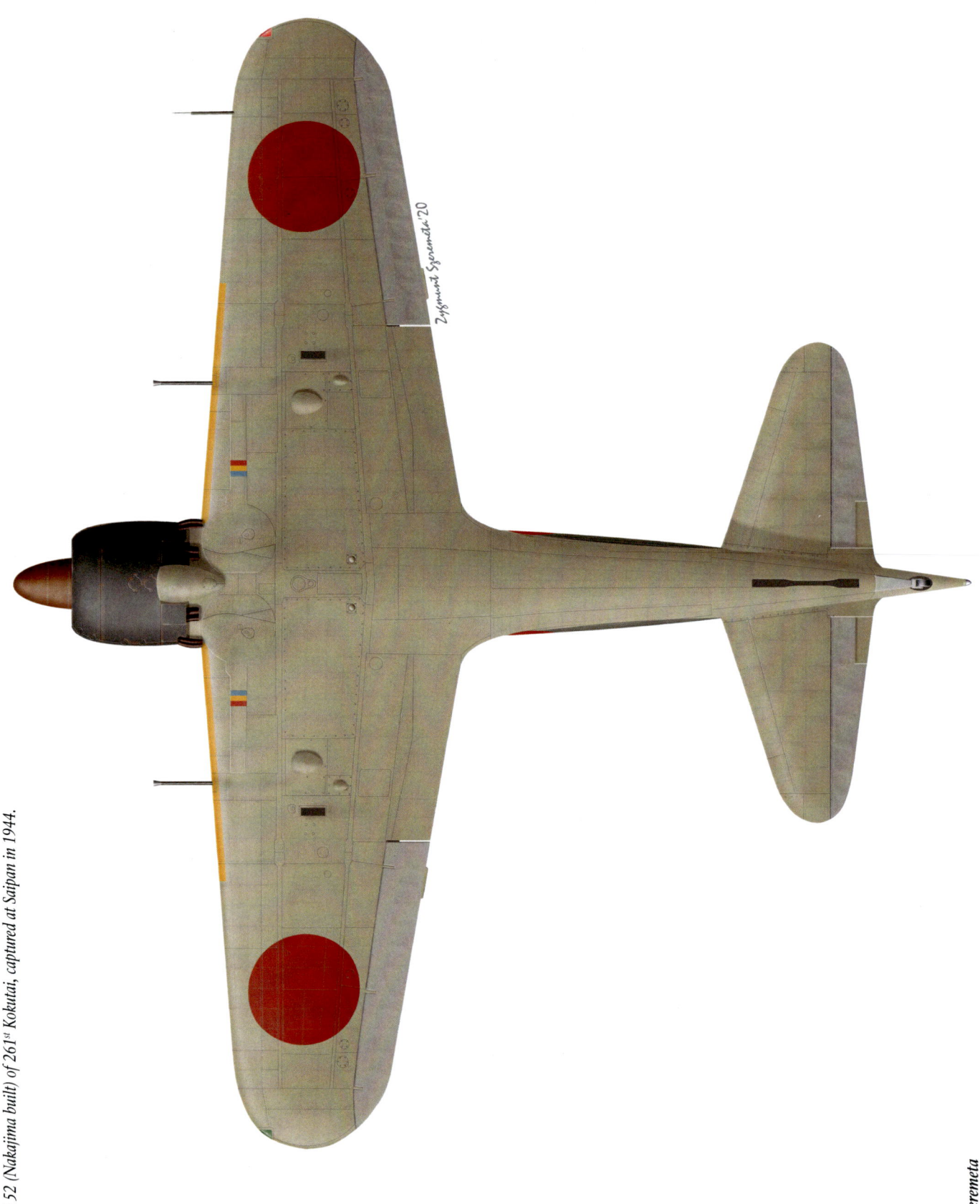

A5M5 Model 52 (Nakajima built) of 261ˢᵗ Kokutai, captured at Saipan in 1944.

Zygmunt Szeremeta